Vince Carter: The Inspiring Story of One of Basketball's Most Dynamic Shooting Guards

An Unauthorized Biography

By: Clayton Geoffreys

Table of Contents

Foreword

No other player is remembered from the 2000 NBA dunk contest than Vince Carter. The stage was set for Vince back in the heyday of the dunk contest when rules were more lax and friendly to classic street-style dunking. No other player is revered as dearly as Vince Carter for his or her 2000 NBA dunk contest performance. Though his cousin, Tracy McGrady, and Houston Rockets star Steve Francis, may have attempted to put on a show, Vince stole the show in 2000. Vince Carter solidified his legacy as one of the best dunk contest competitors in NBA history; but besides that, he has led a storied career in the NBA, full of excitement with his dynamic game. From once being prized as a first option to adjusting his career to fit the needs of his team, Vince Carter has appropriately adapted his playing styles to his respective teams, making him a valuable contributor to any team he has played on. An eight-time NBA All-Star, Carter will go down in history as one of the best shooting guards of the recent era of basketball. Thank you for downloading *Vince Carter: The Inspiring Story of One of Basketball's Most Dynamic Shooting Guards.* In this unauthorized biography, we will learn Vince Carter's incredible life story and impact on the game of basketball. Hope you enjoy and if you do, please do not forget to leave a review! Also, check out my website at claytongeoffreys.com to join my exclusive list where I let you know about my latest books and give you goodies!

Cheers,

Clayton Geoffreys

Visit me at www.claytongeoffreys.com

Introduction

Vince Carter is the greatest dunker of all time.

The 2000 Dunk Contest. The Frederic Weis dunk. When people talk about Vince Carter, they talk about his dunks. How he wowed fans across the world. How he made highlight reel after highlight reel. How every aspiring basketball player dreamed of dunking like Carter. As a 37-year old Vince Carter prepares to enter the final years of his career, everyone is prepared to acclaim him as the greatest dunker in NBA history.

And that acclamation is insulting to Vince Carter.

What people have forgotten about Vince Carter is that he was not just a dunker. James White, who played 67 games in the NBA, was just a dunker. Shannon Brown, who once nearly jumped over a 6'6'' guard in the middle of a playoff game, was just a dunker. Vince Carter was not just a dunker. He was one of the best players in the NBA at his height. He brought basketball to Canada and the young Toronto Raptors.

In his third season in the NBA, he arguably outdueled league MVP Allen Iverson in one of the greatest playoff series in NBA history. Vince was an all-around player who could score from anywhere, pass well for a scoring guard, and led the Toronto Raptors to multiple playoff berths almost completely by himself.

But to win a NBA championship takes some luck, and Vince never got lucky. He never played alongside a truly great teammate in Toronto. Eventually, the Toronto fans perceived him as a quitter and Carter became the most hated player in Raptors history. Carter was traded to the New Jersey Nets and played alongside fellow All-Star Jason Kidd, but the Nets suffered from fatal flaws that prevented playoff success. Later with the Orlando Magic, Carter choked in the 2010 NBA Playoffs at the free throw line. After a miserable season in 2010-11 with the Phoenix Suns, Vince Carter looked finished.

But unlike many aging stars who refuse to accept that their days as a premier player are over, Vince Carter readjusted his career and became a useful role player with the Dallas Mavericks. He contributed to Dallas's return to the playoffs and helped Dallas give the eventual champion San Antonio Spurs their greatest challenge in the 2014 playoffs. For all of his depictions as a human highlight reel, Vince Carter has been just a basketball player, committed to the game and to his team's victory. That is a legacy far more important than any dunk.

Chapter 1: Childhood and Early Life

Vincent Lamont Carter Jr. was born on January 26, 1977 in Daytona Beach, Florida to Michelle and Vince Carter Sr. From the moment of his birth, basketball played a role in the young Vince's life. When he was brought home from the hospital, Vince's father and uncle tossed a little rubber basketball over the baby's crib. When Vince learned to sit up, he began to hold basketballs. By the time he was two-years-old, he was dribbling basketballs. While today's stars grew up worshipping Jordan or Kobe or LeBron, Vince grew up idolizing Julius "Dr. J" Erving. Erving was among the first basketball superstars to turn dunking into an art form for high-flying wings instead of a finishing move for big men. Vince wanted to be just like Dr. J.

When Vince was 7, his parents divorced. Vince's mother Michelle was awarded custody of Vince and his younger brother Chris. Michelle later remarried to Harry Robinson, a fellow co-teacher. Harry got along well with the two boys, and worked to nurture Vince's basketball talents.

Basketball was not all Vince did during his early years. The Carters were an upper middle-class family, and Vince's parents encouraged him into the arts and music. Vince would enjoy his time as a musician and played football for fun. But basketball was his primary passion.

By the time Vince reached 11, he touched the basketball rim for the first time in his career. By age 12, he dunked for the first time. But just like in the NBA, Vince was more than a dunker when playing in the playground. He was bigger than everyone else, and was placed in charge of handling the ball and defending tough opponents.

Chapter 2: High School Years

In 1991, Vince Carter entered Mainland High School, where his stepfather taught band. It was at Mainland High School where Carter showed that he had NBA-level potential. Carter was less than six feet tall in his freshman year, and did not make the varsity team. He became the star of the junior varsity team, and learned to fight the constant double teams that swarmed him. He practiced his jumping ability and also worked on his passing and shooting.

In his sophomore year, Vince made the varsity team and averaged 20 points a game. Carter began to be noticed amongst the local community for his high-flying athleticism, but it was in his junior year when he took off as a high school superstar. Mainland Coach Charles Brinkerhoff moved Carter, who had grown to 6'6'', to the small forward position. Carter took advantage of his size to post up opponents and grab rebounds. He also became a terror on the defensive end as he used his leaping ability to block jump shooters. Everyone in the local community came to see Vince play, and Mainland High School had to place the overflowing crowd in the cafeteria while showing the game through closed circuit television. Vince averaged 25 points and 11 rebounds in his junior year, and Mainland finished with a 30-2 record. They would be eliminated in the semifinals of the 6A Florida State tournament.

In his senior year, Carter declared to the rest of his team that they were going to win the high school championship that year. Mainland went out and did just that, finishing with a 33-2 record and their first basketball title in 56 years. In the semifinals against Miami's Northwestern High, Carter took off from the free throw line and dunked over Miami star center Tim James. James was sent sprawling onto the floor and the crowd erupted into a frenzy. Coach Brinkerhoff said that was the moment when he knew "Vince Carter had arrived." At the end of the season, Carter was named a

McDonald's All-American and Florida's Mr. Basketball.

Outside of the basketball court, Vince was known for his humility and his hard work in fields other than basketball. Vince continued to play band throughout his high school years. His teammates ribbed him for it, but Carter enjoyed it. He primarily played the drums and also learned the saxophone. Carter became so good at band that he was actually offered a music scholarship to the nearby Bethune-Cookman University. Carter also finished high school with a 3.0 grade point average, played on the volleyball team, and dabbled in poetry. Despite his growing talent and national fame, Vince Carter was able to keep basketball in perspective.

But basketball now offered Carter a chance to join universities across the country. Since Carter was a Florida native, many expected that he would join Florida or Florida State. However, Vince Carter decided that he would join the University of North Carolina (UNC) in the fall of 1995. While Carter was sad to leave his native Florida, he believed that UNC offered him the best chance at developing his basketball skills. Carter was now a nation-wide phenomenon and had been placed on the cover of SLAM Magazine. There was no doubt that if he possessed the talent needed to make it into the NBA.

Chapter 3: College Years at the University of North Carolina

Freshman Season:

When Vince Carter entered UNC for the first time, he was greeted with adoration. The North Carolina Tar Heels had just lost its two main stars in Jerry Stackhouse and Rasheed Wallace. They were looking for a new star to lead them to NCAA success. Vince was not North Carolina's only hope, as there was excitement for fellow incoming freshman Antawn Jamison and Nigerian forward Ademola Okujala. However, neither Jamison nor Okujala possessed Carter's overwhelming athleticism.

Despite the high expectations, Carter's freshman year was a disappointment. He had dominated the high school scene largely through his great athleticism, but this advantage was no longer as significant in college. Opposing college defenders were quicker to trap him into the lane, and Vince's effort on defense lapsed, as he grew frustrated on the offensive end. Midway through the college season, UNC coach Dean Smith placed Carter on the bench. While Vince played less than 18 minutes per game and scored just 7.5 points per game, Antawn Jamison won the Atlantic Coast Conference (ACC) Rookie of the Year.

It was a disappointing first season not just for Vince Carter, but also for the Tar Heels. North Carolina finished with a 21-11 record, a significant decline compared to their success last year with Stackhouse and Wallace. They lost in the first round of the ACC tournament and the second round of the NCAA tournament. In their defeat to Texas Tech in the NCAA game, Carter scored 12 points on 7 shots and played 17 minutes.

Carter's disappointing freshman season ultimately proved to be a blessing in disguise. He realized that he would need to adjust his play in order to adapt to the college game. Over the offseason, Carter worked to improve his decision making in order to not get trapped in the paint as had occurred in his freshman year, and did the little things on offense that Coach Smith appreciated. Smith later said in 2010 that Carter's "not great freshman year might have helped him work even harder his sophomore year."

Sophomore Season:

In Carter's sophomore year, Dean Smith decided to move Carter to the small forward slot. Carter preferred playing shooting guard, but he accepted Smith's decision and used his athleticism to bang in the post and grab rebounds. The fact that he was closer to the rim as a small forward meant that he had more opportunities to finish at the rim.

Carter was now the third option on UNC behind Williams and Jamison. He was also routinely switched in and out of the starting lineup with Ademola Okujala depending on the matchup. Despite the lack of consistency, Carter accepted his role without complaint. He became the best perimeter defender on the team, and Coach Smith said that Carter could guard anyone from 5'10'' point guards to 6'9'' power forwards. Carter's ability to finish without his ferocious dunks improved, but he still wowed fans nationwide with windmills and alley-oops. He now possessed an all-around game. Over his sophomore season, Carter averaged 13 points, 4.5 rebounds, 2.4 assists, and 1.4 steals in less than 28 minutes of play.

The developing play of both Carter and Jamison meant that the North Carolina Tar Heels rebounded from last season's disappointment. They improved to a 28-7 record and finished third in the ACC. North Carolina easily won the ACC tournament and earned the #1 seed in the East Regional of the 1997 NCAA Tournament. Carter had two strong games against California in the East Regional Semifinal and Louisville in the East Regional Finals. Against Louisville, Carter scored 18 points on 10 shots and also had 7 rebounds and 5 assists. North Carolina returned to the Final Four for the third time in five years.

North Carolina would face off against Arizona in the Final Four. The Arizona Wildcats were led by a young, promising backcourt of Mike Bibby and Miles Simon. Bibby and Simon eviscerated the North Carolina backcourt of Ed Cota and Shammond Williams. The two Arizona guards combined for 44 points while Cota and Williams scored just 8 points and took 22 shots. Vince Carter led North Carolina throughout the game and finished with 21 points and 6 rebounds. But his efforts were not enough to make up for the huge difference between the two backcourts, and Arizona eliminated North Carolina with a 63-56 victory.

Junior Season:

Carter decided to play for one more season at North Carolina, but everyone was certain that he would enter the NBA after his junior year. Nevertheless, Carter was fully committed to North Carolina. He wanted to leave college with a championship just like he had in high school.

But just as Carter's junior year began, the season was nearly derailed when Coach Dean Smith suddenly announced his retirement on October 9, 1997. The news became a bombshell not just in North Carolina, but in the entire college basketball scene. Smith had coached North Carolina since 1961. He had taught many great players like Michael Jordan, James Worthy, and Rasheed Wallace. But Smith stated that he had lost enthusiasm for the game, and assistant Bill Guthridge took over the head coaching position.

Smith had ran a system of "six starters" during Vince Carter's time with North Carolina, and as noted above frequently placed Carter on the bench when he felt it was needed. Guthridge by contrast wanted Carter to stay in the starting lineup. Guthridge was not as controlling or demanding as Smith was, and preferred to rely on his players' individual brilliance instead of a coaching system.

While such an idea may have seemed risky, North Carolina greatly improved in Vince Carter's junior year. The Tar Heels were bolstered by the arrival of future NBA center Brendan Haywood and the development of Jamison and Carter. Haywood guarded the paint, Carter shut down the opposing team's best player, and Jamison scored. UNC finished with a 34-4 record that season and won the ACC tournament for a second straight year. Carter finished the season improving his averages to 15.6 points on 59% shooting, 5.1 rebounds, and 1.2 steals per game. He was nominated to the Second Team All-American.

In the NCAA tournament, Carter played a key role in North Carolina's wins against UNC-Charlotte and Connecticut. In the latter game, Carter shut down Connecticut star shooting guard Richard "Rip" Hamilton, holding him to just 5-21 shooting for 18 points. For the second straight year, North Carolina found itself in the Final Four. Unfortunately, the Tar Heels came out flat against Utah in the first half and fell behind by 13. Carter led all scorers with 21 points and attempted to spark a rally, but North Carolina still lost 65-59.

Carter was disappointed by North Carolina's failure to win a NCAA championship. While it had been all but assured that he would leave for the NBA after his junior season, Carter now contemplated staying, aiming for a NCAA championship one last time, and graduating with a degree in African studies. However, teammate Shammond Williams was graduating and Jamison declared for the NBA draft. Their decisions provided the final push, as Carter did not want to be stuck carrying a depleted North Carolina team by himself in his senior year. On May 1, 1998, Vince Carter declared for the NBA Draft.

NBA teams were intrigued by Carter's athleticism, potential, and his high-flying dunks. They also liked how his perimeter shooting had improved in his years with North Carolina. On the other hand, they were uncertain about Carter's ball handling and were concerned about his ability to carry a franchise.

On the night of the 1998 NBA Draft, the first three picks went to Michael Olowokandi, Mike Bibby, and Raef LaFrentz. The Toronto Raptors selected Antawn Jamison with the 4th pick and the Golden State Warriors picked Carter with the 5th pick. But just as Carter prepared to put on Golden State's hat, Toronto and Golden State announced that they intended to swap the teammates. The two traded their hats in front of NBA Commissioner David Stern. The Raptors had intended to select Carter all along, but saw an opportunity to sell Jamison to the Warriors for Carter and cash. The seemingly minor trade would have drastic repercussions for the two franchises. Jamison would be just another moment in Golden State's long-suffering history, as he failed to lead Golden State to the playoffs for five seasons before being traded to the Dallas Mavericks. Carter by contrast was about to bring basketball to Canada.

Chapter 4: Carter's NBA Career

The High-Flyer in Toronto

Today, basketball in Canada is more successful than ever. Canadians Anthony Bennett and Andrew Wiggins were selected with the first pick in the 2013 and 2014 NBA Drafts respectively. Before them, Vancouver native Steve Nash wowed the NBA with his "seven seconds and less" offense. Nash won two MVPs and led the Phoenix Suns to multiple trips deep in the playoffs.

But in 1998, the situation could not have been more different. The Toronto Raptors had been created in 1995 as part of a wave of NBA expansion teams in the early 1990s. The NBA had also created another Canadian expansion team in the Vancouver Grizzlies, but both teams struggled in their opening years. Analysts questioned whether Canada could support a NBA team. The Grizzlies proved unable to find a star unwilling to play in Vancouver, and moved to

Memphis, Tennessee in 2001. If a different team had drafted Vince, perhaps Toronto would have undergone the same fate.

As the 1998-99 season began, the Raptors aside from Carter were a mess. Their best player was guard Doug Christie, a defensive specialist who was wholly unsuitable for any offensive role except shooting three-pointers. Other major players were an aging Charles Oakley and Kevin Willis, both whom were above 35. In addition, the 1998-99 season was hampered by a lockout that lasted until January 7. The season was compressed to 50 games, which favored teams that had experience playing together unlike the Raptors.

Still, things were not wholly negative for Carter. The biggest positive was the presence of his cousin Tracy McGrady. McGrady was two years younger than Vince, but had been drafted straight out of high school by the Raptors a year earlier. His playing time had been minimal during his rookie season, but Carter was excited for the chance to play alongside his relative.

On February 5, 1999, Vince Carter made his NBA debut against the Boston Celtics. He scored 16 points on 5-11 shooting, and the Raptors won 103-92. Like most rookies, Carter had consistency issues, but he showed from the beginning his basketball ability. In just his third game, he scored 22 points against the Milwaukee Bucks. On March 25, he scored a season-high 32 points against the Houston Rockets. Carter's performance was punctuated by a 360 dunk, but perhaps the most impressive part was how he repeatedly scored on renowned defender Scottie Pippen in the post. Carter finished his rookie season averaging 18.3 points on 45% shooting, along with 5.7 rebounds, 3 assists, and 1.5 blocks. He led all rookies in scoring.

Carter's numbers were impressive, but what was even better was that these numbers translated into wins for the Raptors. In March, the Raptors had an 11-6 record, the first winning month in franchise history. It seemed that Toronto might make the playoffs, but they faded down the stretch and finished with a 23-27 record and the 10th seed. It was still the highest winning percentage in franchise history. At the end of the season, Vince Carter received the Rookie of the Year award.

Vince Carter's first season was impressive for a rookie, but it was in his second year that "Vinsanity" was born. In the 1999 NBA Draft, the Raptors traded the 5th pick in the draft for veteran power forward Antonio Davis. Davis provided frontcourt help for Carter. Tracy McGrady also began to develop alongside Carter, and averaged over 15 points in the 1999-2000 season.

With the additional help surrounding him, Vince Carter exploded onto the scene. On January 14, 2000, he scored 47 points against the Bucks. On February 27, he scored 51 points against the Phoenix Suns, a NBA season high. Carter electrified fans and analysts with his ferocious dunks, but he also had other weapons. Carter developed a pull-up jumper, improved his ball handling skills so that he could split double teams, and improved his passing. His defensive effort was lacking at times, but that was understandable given the huge offensive burden he had to carry.

That season, Carter was not just nominated to the All-Star Game, but was voted in as a starter. But the All-Star Game would not be the biggest event of that year's All-Star Week. It was the 2000 Slam Dunk Contest that etched Vince's reputation in the masses as a great dunker. The contest was filled with excellent dunkers besides Vince. Houston Rockets guard Steve Francis had also impressed the NBA with his athleticism and Tracy McGrady also participated. McGrady was initially unwilling because he believed he had no chance of beating Carter. Carter had to all but drag his cousin into it.

Carter practiced a series of dunks for the contest, but used none of them on the night of the contest. Instead, on his first dunk he went for something he had never tried – a reverse 360 windmill. He got it right on his very first attempt, and the arena went insane. Stars like Dikembe Mutombo and Shaquille O'Neal jumped about in total disbelief and amazement. But the show was just beginning. On Carter's third dunk attempt, a behind the legs dunk courtesy of a pass from Tracy McGrady, Dunk contest judge and NBA legend Isiah Thomas came over the table to kneel in front of Carter. Steve Francis had some impressive dunks as well and might have won in any other year. But at the end of the night, Vince Carter was the unquestionable winner.

On the basketball court, the Raptors finished the season with a 45-37 record and qualified for the playoffs for the first time in franchise history. They faced the New York Knicks. Carter struggled in his playoff debut, shooting just 3-20 for 16 points. In Game 2, he bounced back and scored 27 points, but for the first time encountered an issue that would plague him for the rest of his career. With 10 seconds to go, New York guard Latrell Sprewell hit a fade away shot over Carter to give New York the 84-83 lead. On the last possession of the game, Carter received the ball and passed it to a wide-open Dee Brown. Brown missed the jump shot and the Knicks won. Despite his overall game, Carter was questioned for his unwillingness to take the final shot. It would not be the last time that people would wonder about his ability in the clutch. The Knicks would go on to win Game 3 and sweep the series. Despite the playoff defeat, the 1999-2000 season had been a resounding success for Carter, who was nominated to the All-NBA Third Team.

The 2000 offseason would be eventful for Vince Carter. Raptors coach Butch Carter was replaced with Hall of Fame player and coach Lenny Wilkens. Wilkens brought a calming presence to the Toronto locker room and inspired respect from everyone. On a less positive note, Tracy McGrady decided to sign with the Orlando Magic that offseason. McGrady would eventually become a superstar with the Magic. If he had chosen to stay with the Raptors, perhaps he could have been the star player who Vince Carter never played with in his Toronto years.

Vince Carter was also selected to play for the United States in the 2000 Olympics in Sydney. He was the youngest player on the team. On September 25, 2000, the United States faced France as part of the group stage. In the second half, Carter stole the ball. He challenged 7'2'' French center Frederic Weis and jumped over the center, slamming the ball. The French media dubbed it *le dunk de la mort* – "the dunk of death." The dunk over Weis is arguably Carter's most famous dunk of all. The United States would later prevail over France in the gold medal game.

As the 2000-01 season began, the Raptors tried to build a supporting cast around Carter. They brought in rebounder Keon Clark, point guard Chris Childs, and rookie Morris Peterson. Carter continued to be a ferocious dunker and continually took it to the rim, but he also began to rely more on his jumper. He shot nearly 41% from the three-point line that season, which meant that opposing defenders had to be wary of Carter no matter where he was. That season, Carter averaged a career-high 27.6 points per game on 46% shooting. He went to the All-Star game for a second straight year along with teammate Antonio Davis and was nominated to the All-NBA second team. The Raptors improved to win 47 games and finished with the 5th seed in the Eastern Conference.

In the first round of the 2001 NBA Playoffs, the Raptors matched up against the New York Knicks once again. New York had changed dramatically over the past year. Legend Patrick Ewing had been traded and guards Latrell Sprewell and Allan Houston now led the team. Both Knicks guards were capable defenders, and they harassed Carter throughout the series. Carter struggled badly in the first three games, and the Knicks took the 2-1 lead in the best of five series. But in Games 4 and 5, Carter took over. He scored 32 points to lead Toronto to a 100-93 win over the Knicks. In Game 5 in Madison Square Garden, Carter scored 27 points. With 1:30 left in the fourth quarter and the Raptors leading 85-83, Carter missed a difficult floater over Charlie Ward. However, Carter raced to rebound his own miss and laid the ball in to give Toronto a two-possession lead. The Raptors prevailed 93-89 and advanced to the second round. It was their first playoff series win in franchise history.

The next series became one of the great duels in NBA history. Vince Carter and the Raptors took on Allen Iverson and the Philadelphia 76ers. Iverson was the league MVP that season and had scored over 31 points per game that season. He also had key defensive players like Eric Snow and Defensive Player of the Year Dikembe Mutombo who would make scoring difficult for Vince Carter. But Carter knew that if the

Raptors wanted to win the series, he would have to outplay Iverson.

In Game 1, Carter struck first. Iverson did outscore Carter 36 to 35 for the game. However, Carter took 29 shots to score 35 as opposed to Iverson's 34. And just like the Game 5 victory over the Knicks, Carter missed a floater in the final seconds, but grabbed the rebound and laid the ball in to secure Toronto's 96-93 victory. Iverson struck back in Game 2 with 54 points to lead Philadelphia to the win. In Game 3 in Toronto, Carter answered with 50 points. He set a NBA record with 8 straight made three-pointers. In Game 5, Iverson scored 52 points after receiving the MVP trophy. After Toronto won Game 6, the series was tied at three games apiece. The deciding Game 7 would be held in Philadelphia.

However, the last game would be marred by a decision from Vince Carter. In the summer of 2000, Carter had finished up the final credits needed to earn his bachelor's degree from North Carolina. However, North Carolina's graduation ceremony was set on the same date as Game 7. Carter flew down to Chapel Hill, North Carolina, received his degree wearing cap and gown, and then flew back to Philadelphia for Game 7. Perhaps because of his decision to receive his graduation, Carter had a bad Game 7 and shot just 6-18 from the field. With 2 seconds left in the game, Toronto was down 88-87 and had the ball. Point guard Dell Curry inbounded the ball to Carter, who faked a shot to get the Philadelphia defender into the air, took the potential game winner…and watched as it clanged off the rim. The 76ers would win and move on to face the Milwaukee Bucks in the Eastern Conference Finals. Carter would be criticized for his decision to attend his graduation. One NBA player noted how such a decision undoubtedly threw off Vince Carter's routine – a risky move given the importance of Game 7.

The Fall of Vinsanity

In the summer of 2001, Carter signed an extension with the Raptors for six years and $94 million. He was one of the most popular NBA athletes in the world, had revitalized a dormant Toronto franchise, and was just 24 years old. It seemed that Carter would stay a Raptor for many years, and could one day lead them to a championship.

What no one knew was that Vince Carter had already achieved his peak. Carter's high-flying athletic style was not without risk. It placed a great deal of strain on his legs and knees. Out of a desire to preserve his long-term health, Carter became less aggressive on the offensive and defensive end. He shot more jumpers and drove to the rim less than he used to. In the 2001-02 season, his scoring dropped from 27.6 points on 46% shooting to 24.7 points on 43% shooting.

While Carter's performance regressed, the Raptors struggled for most of the season. Aside from picking up a fading Hakeem Olajuwon, Toronto had not improved Carter's supporting cast. Vince missed the 2002 All-Star Game due to his continuing knee and leg problems, and in March decided to undergo arthroscopic knee surgery. Toronto at that point was below .500 and was unlikely to make the playoffs. But to everyone's surprise, the Raptors closed the season by winning 12 of their final 14 games and secured the 7th seed. Carter was unavailable to play for the playoffs, but the Raptors behind Keon Clark and Antonio Davis were able to force the Pistons to five games before losing in the first round. Toronto's relative success meant that sports analysts and fans began to question Vince and how much he meant to a winning team.

Perhaps Vince could have quelled these accusations by rebounding back to his old form in the 2002-03 season. Instead, he regressed even more and his injury problems continued. Carter played just 43 games that season, and his scoring dropped to 20 points a game.

The Raptors won just 24 games that season. Back in 1998, Toronto had essentially selected Vince Carter with the 4th pick with the hope that Carter would keep them out of the lottery. Now five years later, the Raptors once again had the 4th pick in the draft. They selected power forward Chris Bosh.

The Raptors attempted to rebuild in 2003-04, and brought in players like Jalen Rose and Donyell Marshall. Toronto stayed around the .500 mark for the first half of the season, but injuries to Carter and other key Raptor players caused Toronto to collapse once again. Carter averaged 22.5 points and played 73 games, but played hobbled for much of the second half of the season.

The relationship between Carter and the Raptors had grown rocky due to the lack of success. By 2004-05 it completely broke down. Sam Mitchell became the new coach of the Toronto Raptors. Mitchell was an incredibly tough coach who believed in team ball. He clashed with Vince and stated that he believed that Carter spent too much time in the training room. Carter reportedly even tangled with Mitchell and slammed his coach onto the training room floor!

It was clear by the beginning of the season that the Raptors and Carter had to go their separate ways. On December 18, 2004, Vince Carter was traded to the New Jersey Nets for Alonzo Mourning, a few picks, and various other players. The Raptors never really recovered from losing their franchise player, and have yet to get past the first round of the playoffs in the nine years since the Carter trade.

The New Jersey Years:

In acquiring Vince Carter, the New Jersey Nets were seeking a way to reload and retool. Under superstar point guard Jason Kidd, the Nets had been made the NBA Finals in 2002 and 2003. But after losing in the second round of the playoffs in 2004, All-Star forward Kenyon Martin had signed with the Denver Nuggets.

In acquiring Carter, the Nets wanted to show Kidd that they were committed to building a winning team.

Revitalized by moving to a new franchise, Carter had his best season in years. In 2004-05, he nearly equaled his 2000-01 statistical peak. He scored above 40 points in 5 games that season, and averaged 27.5 points on 46% shooting along with 5.9 rebounds and 4.7 assists with the Nets. On April 15, 2005, Carter played his first game back in Toronto. Raptors fans had been enraged by what they perceived as Carter quitting on the Raptors in his final days and booed him with gusto. Carter said nothing back, but responded with 39 points and 17 in the third quarter. The Nets won 101-90.

New Jersey finished with a 42-40 record that season and faced the Miami Heat in the first round of the NBA playoffs. However, Carter struggled against rising Heat guard Dwyane Wade. Carter averaged 26.8 points for the series, but shot just 36% from the field and 31% from three. New Jersey was swept in four games, and Vince's ability to perform in the playoffs was again called into doubt.

Over the next two seasons, Carter and the Nets had some successes, reaching the second round of the playoffs in both seasons. But while Kidd was an excellent point guard and Carter a strong swingman, New Jersey's frontcourt depth was abysmal. Bit players like Jason Collins, Mikki Moore and Brian Scalabrine played significant minutes for the Nets at the power forward and center slots. This weakness prevented the Nets from seriously contending for a championship, and New Jersey was eliminated by Miami in 2006 and Cleveland in 2007. Carter had his moments, such as an excellent performance against the Raptors in the first round of the 2007 playoffs and a vicious dunk on center Alonzo Mourning in 2005. But he was nowhere close to winning a championship.

In the 2007-2008 season, the Nets decided to trade an aging Kidd to the Dallas Mavericks for younger guard

Devin Harris. It was clear that New Jersey intended to rebuild, but they made no attempt to move Carter. Even though the aging Carter found himself on a team which was no longer aiming for the playoffs, he did not complain or ask for a trade. New Jersey asked that Carter stay and serve as a role mentor to young players like Ryan Anderson and Brook Lopez. Carter served in that role for the next two seasons, waiting to be sent to a championship team. In 2008, he failed to make the All-Star team for the first time in seven years.

Is This the End?

On June 25, 2009, the trade finally came. Carter was sent to his hometown Orlando Magic to play with rising superstar center Dwight Howard. The Magic had just lost in the NBA Finals, and were seeking a wingman to pair with Howard like Clyde Drexler had with Olajuwon and Kobe had with Hakeem.

Orlando had excellent depth, and so Carter played a career low 30.8 minutes per game that season. He averaged a career-low 16.6 points and 3.9 rebounds on 43% shooting. Carter still had big games such as a 48-point performance against the New Orleans Hornets, and the Magic won 59 games and earned the second seed in the East. They swept the first two rounds of the playoffs against the Charlotte Bobcats and the Atlanta Hawks. For the first time in his career, Vince Carter made it past the second round of the playoffs.

The Magic faced the Boston Celtics in the Eastern Conference Finals. After playing well in the first two rounds, Carter was a disaster against the tough Celtics defense. In Game 2, the Magic were down 95-92 with 31 seconds left. Carter was fouled, and went to the free throw lines with the game on the line. Even though Carter was an 84% free throw shooter that season, he missed both of them. The Celtics went on to win Game 2, and defeated the Magic in six games.

The Magic were frustrated by Carter's performance against the Celtics, and began to look for another swingman. On December 18, 2010, Carter was traded to the Phoenix Suns. Phoenix had little interest in Vince Carter. They traded not for Carter the player, but for Carter's expiring contract of over $10 million in order to get out of the bigger deal for Hedo Turkoglu. After one ineffective season with the Suns in which he missed the playoffs, the Suns waived Carter in December 2011.

From All-Star to Role Player

Vince Carter was 34 years old, had not made the All-Star team since 2007, and had watched his legendary athleticism slowly decline. Many NBA superstars would have chosen to retire at that point, but Carter wanted to stay in the NBA. Shortly after being waived from the Suns, Carter signed with the Dallas Mavericks. The Mavericks were the defending NBA champions, but few expected them to defend their title after they let key center Tyson Chandler go to the New York Knicks. Carter could not make up for the departure of Chandler, but he could serve as a scoring punch to complement Dirk Nowitzki.

Vince Carter no longer ferociously dunked the ball like he had in the past, but his all-around skills made him a valuable contributor for Dallas. Vince's perimeter shooting was among his best skills, as his defender could not double Dirk Nowitzki on the post. If they did, Dirk would pass the ball to a wide-open Vince Carter standing on the three-point line. Dallas Coach Rick Carlisle moved Carter in and out of the lineup to find the best rotation for the team. When Carter was benched and did not play alongside Dirk, he would then use his ball handling to get to the rim and finish. He laid the ball more often than he dunked, but two points are two points.

Carter played well enough in the 2011-12 season that the Mavericks decided to keep him around for another year. With another year playing alongside Dirk and Carlisle, Vince revitalized his career. Long-time

Mavericks shooting guard Jason Terry had left during the offseason for the Boston Celtics. For the past four seasons, Terry had played the part of a sixth man to come off the bench and score while Dirk rested. Coach Carlisle decided to give that role to Vince. Vince Carter would start only three games during the 2012-13 season, and zero in 2013-14.

Vince could have perceived Carlisle's decision for him to come off the bench as an insult, but he took it in stride. Over the next two seasons, Vince Carter revitalized his career. His perimeter shooting in particular improved, as he shot around 40% from three-point range in both seasons. He averaged 13.4 points in the 2012-13 season, and 11.9 points in 2013-14.

The Dallas Mavericks narrowly missed the playoffs in 2012-13 because Nowitzki missed 27 games due to knee surgery, but managed to grab the eighth seed in 2014. They found themselves up against the San

Antonio Spurs. The Spurs were a team on a mission to avenge their devastating 2013 NBA Finals defeat to the Miami Heat. They won 62 games that season, the best in the league. Everyone expected the Spurs to easily sweep Dallas.

Instead, the Mavericks gave San Antonio the fight of their lives. After losing Game 1, Dallas blew out San Antonio 113-92 in Game 2. The series returned to Dallas. In Game 3, the Spurs and Mavericks battled back and forth with both teams taking the lead. Late in the game, Spurs guard Manu Ginobili hit the layup to put San Antonio ahead 108-106 with 1.7 seconds left. Who was the ball going to go to? The Spurs would cover Dirk heavily. Dallas's main guard Monta Ellis is a poor three-point shooter. Late in the game, the ball fell into the hands of Vince Carter.

It was almost an exact microcosm of that moment 13 years ago, when Carter missed a three point shot that would have taken his Toronto Raptors to the Eastern

Conference Finals. He got the ball at almost the exact same spot, pump faked and drew the Spurs defender into the air just like then, and fired a fade-away three pointer. The only difference was that this time, the shot went in. Dallas won 109-108. Vince Carter was mobbed by his teammates, coaches, and Dallas owner Mark Cuban.

The Mavericks would eventually lose to the Spurs in seven games, though Vince Carter would shoot nearly 48% from three-point range over the series. However, they were the only team to force the eventual champions to seven games. Just a few years ago, it appeared that Vince Carter's days in the NBA were numbered. But for that one game, the Vinsanity of old was back.

Chapter 5: Vince's Personal Life

Vince Carter may have been an incredible basketball player, but he has always been able to keep the sport in perspective. Other players like Bill Russell, Kobe Bryant, and Michael Jordan have been homicidally obsessed with victory. While Carter undoubtedly seeks a NBA championship, he understands that no matter how great one is at basketball, it is just a game. Perhaps Carter could be criticized for his lack of will compared to Jordan; on the other hand, one could say that Vince is just a better-rounded individual.

Family has been one of the most important things in Vince's life. When Vince Carter was drafted to the NBA, he immediately used his money to establish The Embassy of Hope, a charitable non-profit that helps the homeless and families in need. His mother helps to manage the charity. One of the points of contention between Vince and the Toronto Raptors in his final season was that Toronto ended a policy of granting his mother a parking spot in the Air Canada Centre. The Raptors wanted to implement a team-based policy in which all players would be treated equally, but Vince's mother used the spot to facilitate her son's charity work.

One avenue that Vince has paid a great deal of attention to is education. His mother was a teacher, and determined to make sure that he graduated from college. It was that determination which led to Vince Carter's controversial decision to attend his graduation on the same day as Game 7. In 2010, Vince Carter returned to UNC to celebrate the school's 100th year anniversary of its basketball program. He played a charity game with fellow alumni and talked about how wonderful it was to be back in UNC. In addition to his college, Carter donated $2.5 million to Mainland High School for the construction of a new gym. In appreciation of Vince's contribution, Mainland erected a life-size statue of Carter in front of the gym.

Chapter 6: Impact on Basketball

As noted above, when people think about Vince Carter, they discuss his dunks. Carter was a creative, high-flying dunker who could wow even the most jaded basketball veterans. As his career prepares to end, everyone is prepared to give him the title as the greatest dunker of all time, above all-time greats like Jordan, Julius Erving, and Dominique Wilkins.

But no matter how spectacular or creative a dunk is, a dunk will always be worth two points. There is in fact another facet of Carter's game that is worthy of analysis, both for how it affected the perception of Carter's career and how it affects how we look at NBA players today. Despite Carter's great athleticism and jump shooting, despite the fact that he was at one point viewed as one of the best shooting guards in the game, media figures have consistently stated that Carter was not clutch. He failed to execute in big games. In 2001, he missed a potential series winner. In the 2005 playoffs, he struggled badly in the Miami sweep. In 2010, he missed two free throws that caused his Orlando Magic to lose a huge playoff game.

All of those moments may seem to show that Vince Carter was not a clutch player, but there is a question that must be asked first: what does it mean to be clutch? It is true that Vince Carter performed worse in the playoffs than in the regular season. However, that is true of practically all players in the postseason, as they must now face tougher and more motivated defenses. Furthermore, Carter did have moments when he hit big shots down the stretch. As noted above, Carter had two layups in the 2001 playoffs which secured the Toronto victory against New York and Philadelphia. Carter had moments where he performed well down the stretch of big games, and he had moments where he struggled. The reality is that is true of all players – not even Jordan hit every attempted game winner.

If we are to analyze Vince Carter's flaws, one should look beyond vague statements like "Vince Carter was not clutch" and instead examine actual flaws in Carter's game. Ironically for the greatest dunker of all time, Vince Carter's problem was that he did not dunk enough. After his peak in 2000-01, Carter began to rely more and more on his perimeter game and jump shot. This style of play has helped to prolong his career, especially in Dallas where his shooting made him an excellent role player. On the other hand, it limited his efficiency and consistency. On some nights, Carter's jump shot would work and he would look like the best shooting guard in the league. On other nights, it did not and he would look like he did not even belong in the NBA. The best guards in the NBA history have all been known for their ability to get and finish at the rim. Carter was perhaps more capable of this than anyone else, but chose not to.

Carter's unwillingness to finish at the rim can be explained partially by the physical burden which superstar wings must bear in the NBA. Carter suffered from a variety of lingering knee and leg issues throughout his career thanks to his playing style. He was frequently criticized for a supposed lack of toughness, but Carter has played at least 60 games in all but one season in his career. He has endured a great deal of pain over his career. One example is that when he was with the Raptor, he suffered a kidney stone during the season. Kidney stones are one of the most painful conditions known to man, and doctors expected Carter to rest after the stone was removed. Instead, Carter was at practice the same day.

Basketball is a physical sport, and the NBA's history is littered with gifted players who were unable to fulfill their potential because of injuries. Vince's cousin Tracy McGrady was essentially finished by the time he reached 30, though he lingered on in the NBA for a few more years. While Carter's style of play prevented him from becoming as good as he could have been, perhaps it has also helped to prolong his career. And while Vince might have taken too many perimeter shots, the fact is that he was devoted to basketball and willing to lead the teams in the playoffs like he did in his early Toronto years.

Chapter 7: Vince Carter's Legacy and Future

Today, Vince Carter is 37 years old. He will be among the oldest players in the league. Furthermore, while some older players like Steve Nash and Kevin Garnett have one foot out of the NBA, Carter has revitalized himself into a useful role player. On July 12, 2014, Carter signed a multi-year deal with the Memphis Grizzlies. The 2014-15 season will be Carter's 16th season in the NBA.

While there were better NBA players during Vince Carter's time, few energized fans as much as he did. In the aftermath of Jordan's retirement in 1998, the league wanted someone who could take over Michael's spot as a high-flying dunker. In that role, Vince arguably surpassed Michael. His dunk over Frederic Weis, his 200 Slam Dunk Contest performance, and countless other dunks are still watched online and adored today.

Carter did not just make the NBA exciting again for old fans, but helped to bring basketball to Canada. While he was raised in Florida, Carter's high-flying dunks and athleticism made basketball cool in Canada. Just like a young Carter was inspired by Julius Erving to play basketball, today's young Canadian athletes have cited Carter as a key influence in their interest in the sport. Tristan Thompson, selected with the 4th pick in the 2010 draft, recalled that watching Vince Carter's highlights made him "fall in love with the game" and told Vince that he was "his Jordan." Boston Celtics prospect Kelly Olynyk remembered how everyone in Canada loved Vince at one point.

Carter excited casual fans, but it should always be remembered that he was so much more. He has lasted 16 years and ranks 25th in NBA history in total points scored. He led the Raptors to multiple trips to the playoffs, including one amazing battle against Allen Iverson. If Carter had a weakness, it was that he did not attempt to dunk enough and relied too much on his jump shot. However, that weakness would permit him to last in the NBA even after his athleticism has declined. The now accurate jump shooter has become a valued role player.

How much longer will Vince Carter be able to last in the NBA? No one knows. But when he finally hangs his shoes up and walks away, we should take care to remember everything he did throughout his career. Not just as a dunker, but as one of the best shooting guards in the history of the game.

Final Word/About the Author

I was born and raised in Norwalk, Connecticut. Growing up, I could often be found spending many nights watching basketball, soccer, and football matches with my father in the family living room. I love sports and everything that sports can embody. I believe that sports are one of most genuine forms of competition, heart, and determination. I write my works to learn more about influential athletes in the hopes that from my writing, you the reader can walk away inspired to put in an equal if not greater amount of hard work and perseverance to pursue your goals. If you enjoyed *Vince Carter: The Inspiring Story of One of Basketball's Most Dynamic Shooting Guards* please leave a review! Also, you can read more of my works on *LeBron James, Kyrie Irving, Klay Thompson, Anthony Davis, Stephen Curry, Kevin Durant, Russell Westbrook, Chris Paul, Blake Griffin, Joakim Noah, Scottie Pippen, Kobe Bryant, Carmelo Anthony, Kevin Love, Grant Hill, Tracy McGrady, Patrick Ewing, Karl*

Malone, Tony Parker, Allen Iverson, Hakeem Olajuwon, Reggie Miller, Michael Carter-Williams, James Harding, John Wall, Tim Duncan, and *Steve Nash* in the Kindle Store. If you love basketball, check out my website at claytongeoffreys.com to join my exclusive list where I let you know about my latest books and give you lots of goodies.

Like what you read?

If you love books on life, basketball, or productivity, check out my website at claytongeoffreys.com to join my exclusive list where I let you know about my latest books. Aside from being the first to hear about my latest releases, you can also download a free copy of *33 Life Lessons: Success Principles, Career Advice & Habits of Successful People.* See you there!

Made in the USA
Middletown, DE
01 March 2016